Eyelid Lick

Published in the United States by Fence Books, Science Library 320, University at Albany, 1400 Washington Avenue, Albany, NY 12222, www.fenceportal.org

Fence Books is a project of Fence Magazine, Incorporated, which is funded in part by support from the New York State Council on the Arts and the National Endowment for the Arts, along with the generous sponsorship of the New York State Writers Institute and the University at Albany. Many thanks to these friends and to all Friends of Fence.

Fence Books are distributed by Consortium Book Sales & Distribution (cbsd.com) and Small Press Distribution (spdbooks.org)

and printed in Canada by The Prolific Group. (prolific.ca)

Cover illustration by Donald Dunbar
Design by Fence Books

Library of Congress Cataloguing in Publication Data
Dunbar, Donald
Eyelid Lick/ Donald Dunbar

Library of Congress Control Number: 2012950437
ISBN 13: 978-1-934200-63-6

FIRST EDITION
10 9 8 7 6 5 4 3 2

Thanks to the editors of 1913: a journal of forms, Draft: the journal of process, > kill author, Octopus, The Oregonian, PEN Poetry Series, *and* Portland Review *for publishing poems from this book, and thanks to the editors who have published my other work, to the curators who have given me spaces to read in, and to my friends and teachers and family. I love you, and feel grateful for your help and company.*

Eyelid Lick

donald dunbar
2012 fence modern poets series

FENCE BOOKS
ALBANY NEW YORK

AUTHOR'S NOTE

The title of this book was *Trust School*. It was supposed to be a textbook for a fictional "trust school"—trust falls, careless cellphone trading, students making love in a brightly lit, all-school assembly—framed by an extremely allegorical story. Actually, I had been writing poems and calling them *Gardenia Trust School*, and each poem first asked the reader to learn how to trust again, and then begged her to trust me. In my head I called this *The Project*, and it was a complete success, but eventually I grew more concerned with the story than the instruction, I had really found the heart of the book, and all the words were beat out by this heart one by one, but by this time it was very dry, and very old, and ruined, and was called *Shooting American Pets*.

Imagine, if you will, a girl named "Copelyn." We'll flesh her out later. She's older now, but she's just enrolled in Trust School! Her teacher is very excited to have such a young woman in the class, such a studious young woman, her teacher is very excited to read to her from *Shoot the Pet*—Chapter 1: There's something new in its whimper.

Minton Sr., her teacher, asks her to give her report: and she does: The book that was eventually written is *No, No, No: An Anthology of Refusal*, a fundamentally stupid memoir about the slow pull of iterations—from teacher to student, from student into teacher—and weeping noises—similar to sounds a kid makes pretending to know another language—and Minton Sr.'s happy marriage to "CC," and titled *Masters & Masters*. There were only two reasons to read it:

1) It was thoroughly true
2) "Lynne Cross," the main character, was modeled on a woman
    your father had once fallen in love with.

You'd never been told about her, but you totally understand, perfectly in fact, because as she's being introduced to you, you, yourself, brush your hand through her hair and kiss her! And that's just not something you do!

Sadly, right as you're really falling for her, and really getting into the book, "Copelyn Cross" meets Fe Hu Chan, and falls in love.

There is nothing more boring than love.

This book is really fucking boring, but Fe Hu Chan, master of Yin-style Baguazhang, thinks you might like it.

And he's basically you.

Let's make him, for just right now, you.

You're quite a guy!

You remind me of a young lady I know: she's thirteen, making love with the whole city, basically, she's just something in the air.

Getting back to basics, "Carolyn" is overdue for real character development. Sure she's older now, but what does that mean? Hoping you'll be impressed, she reads you her reading list from when she was thirteen, but it's awful. *Perfume Tastes Awful*, by Fe Hu Chan, *Macular Hole*, by Fe Hu Chan, *Ashes Grammar* by Fe Hu Chan. Some titles, you suspect, she just made up, but you choose to trust her, out of pity, regardless, because I ask you to.

Usually, a book is about something very particular.

And you're told a lot about it.

I should be horrified, but I'm not sure what we're talking about. Really, there's too much unsaid in this book, or half-said, or said too many times, *way* too much. The full extent becomes apparent when you attempt to read an earlier page and the entire text deforms, as if tied to the slowly turning wheels of a large clock. The true extent, though, to which vagueness and uncertainty are overused only becomes apparent when one wants to go find something one's already read. The entire text deforms—as if the face of it has been scraped off and is beginning to scab over.

It's funny, but sometimes you barely remember her.

In *The Collected Letters*, one of the better comedic sequences involves "Caitlin," the protagonist, trading places with a page in the table of contents, though for the most part the comedy flops. You almost get the sense that the comedy often works, but then sometimes it really does!

One of the most thrilling moments in the book is when "Cloe" reads the list of books she read in high school into a microphone situated somewhere directly below *Calling Card* in your hands. It's almost the sensation of reading out loud it seems so unnatural! Because on one hand you're moving your tongue, but then there's your lips pursing and you have your vocal cords at times engaged, or stretching as if filled with someone else's voice box.

The general effect is warming, and/or threatening, and the perspicuity with which one memory of the words—that is, the sound of them—disagrees with another, and then another still, so that you're remembering things that haven't happened four or five times out," Minton Sr. says.

He catches his reflection in the students' eyes as he walks away from the podium.

Had he always been so dry, so old?

On the specially prepared bed, one of the figures puts her hand on the other's chest. The murmuring is evaporating all around them.

"I notice your eyes," Fe Hu Chan says, "they are glittering."

"I notice my own eyes," says Celia, and hugs onto him, and kisses the side of his mouth, and smiles in his ear, *"all the fucking time!"*

4

[

there is a drawing of a hand here
palm-up, uncalloused fingers

]

table of CONTENTS

I was prophesied to die at a certain age, and knew nothing that could cure me. Later, much later, the world was stretched out before me like some bleached fucking leather, one morning after another. I asked the wise among my friends, "I will go out onto the white and endless savanna, is it there I will find my charm against sleep?" My wise friends consulted one another, and they asked of me eight tasks.

I. I am to go the fountain in town and put into it some of my blood, in the way I would talk with you or write.

2. I will plant lines of rice in such a way that the paddy will grow into a palace.

3. For my third task, I will solve problems such as chemical spills, oil spills, etc.

4. I will find some way to herd the impala, and domesticate them then, perhaps through patience and repetition. In the morning I will pet them on their faces, and in the evening I will pet them on their faces. I will feed them, and wait with them, and pet them on their faces.

5. GOTO 7.

6.

7. I will draw a perfectly round O, or trick something into doing this for me.

8. GOTO 4.

"So you have given up on Duty," my wise friend remarked. "That is a first step."

`A man walks into a bar and orders a drink.
The bartender says, "We're out of drinks.
I'll go get some more. Wait here."

So the bartender goes and the man waits.
It's early afternoon, and not all that nice outside,
plus he's got nowhere else to be. But then

it's late afternoon, and soon it's evening-time.
Other patrons enter the bar, but the man warns them off.
"You go on ahead," he says, "I've got to wait here."

A priest,
a rabbi,
and a momentary lack of judgment walk into a bar

and pay their whole lives
for the crimes of a few minutes.

A duck, a dog, and a Marine Lieutenant
dress up like

an Iraqi, the Pope, and this half-gay four-year-old
and walk into a bar

and the bartender is Jesus Christ.
"What's with the cross?"

asks the Pope, obviously inebriated.
"What's with the," the wounded Christ says

                         "what's with . . . "

The Pope, Billy Graham, and Oral Roberts
chew fingers off of inmates in Virginia.
What's with that?

Two men walk into a bar, and the first man is snuffed out while his mother is shackled to a bed with a sheet up so she can't see the baby she just gave birth to. "What'll you have?"

"I'll have

plastic bags filled with feces and urine dumped all over the sleeping man and his bed."

So the deputy says, " . . . I didn't hear you say 'please.'"

A man walks into a bar and wakes up
in a waterbed. The bartender is sweeping
a dust-rag over the bar and coos, "Good morning,
lil' lamby, it's wake-up time." The alarm is

going off, but the man orders an imported beer
rolls onto his side
and tucks the sheets over his face. The bed
rocks him back and forth
like in the arms of radio waves. "What'll you

have?" the announcer seems to ask.

"I told you," the man mumbles, "an
imported beer and a *butfor*." "What's
a *butfor*?" the bartender asks.

"It's for pooping," the man says.

"Do you have to poop?" asks the bartender, cleaning out a mug with his rag.

"Uh," the man says, "yes."

The bartender squints at the man. "Do you have to poop?" he says.

"Yes," the man says, sort of spelling it out, "yes, I have to poop."

"Do you have to poop? Do you have to poop? Do you have to poop?" the bartender chants, his eyes filling with tears.

Now the man is *really* embarrassed.

"Do You Have To Poop

"Do You Have To Poop" the bartender's eyes are throbbing now, he smashes the mug on the bar and shards fly everywhere, "DO YOU HAVE TO POOP" and the baby in the other room is wrinkly and pink and is moaning and whining

"DO YOU HAVE TO POOP DO YOU HAVE TO POOP" the helicopter's blades get tangled in the power lines and make a sickening thack thack sound and the goldfish goes

POP

and there's a little egg of blood just *floating* there,

in the fishbowl,

and the little girl

cannot find breath to scream.

A fish walks into a bar and asks for a glass of water.
I saw it. It was weird.

A man walks into a bar and asks if they've got any helicopter-flavored potato chips.
"No, we've just got plane."
A man walks into an airport bar and orders a round for all the assholes.
"What'll you have?" asks the bartender.
"No," the man says, "What'll *you* have?"
"Oh," the bartender says, "I'm all set. I've got what I need. It's like, I have friends. I have a few close ones, and a lot of just-close ones.

"It's easy to connect with people, but you wonder if they humor you, if you entertain them.

"I'm scared I like my friends too much. I'm scared I could love them to where they get bored of me. I'm scared it's the idea of me that they like, that I'm the stain of an older, dead me.

"The longer I have a friend the more I worry that. I feel ugly, uglier."

Thirty black guys and a man shot for sport in Virginia walk into an airplane hangar. An inmate's head is stomped on until he soils himself, and that's the happy hour special. "I'll have what she's having," the bartender says, looking at his girlfriend dressed up like a deputy.

The baby starts ringing behind the bar,
so the man, bored and thirsty,

picks it up.
"Hello?" he says into the baby, "I'm not the bartender . . . "

Happy hour, and if you buy one beer you get a glass of pig's blood for free. Jesus walks into a pig pen with a captive bolt pistol and then opts instead to use the powder-actuated nail gun. The prisoners are crawling over each other and sweating and squealing every prayer they've ever learned, but none of these will work. "Please," they beg, "*please*."

A man walks into a bar just after he's pleasured his wife. "You sure look proud of yourself," the bartender says as he pushes the man's face down onto the antique wooden bar and lines up the nail gun to the junction of the brain and the brain stem, "what's with that smile?"

"My wife," the man says, grimacing at his own reflection in the immaculate and tear-streaked wood, "came so hard her cries shattered all the beer mugs."

"That's nothing," says the bartender,

POP

A Mexican, a European, and a Virginian walk into a bar and see a man wearing a robe and sandals turning water into pig's blood.

The Mexican crosses himself, and gets down on one knee, and orders a pint.

The European, figuring it out, also crosses himself, and gets down on one knee, and orders a flight.

The Virginian looks at these other two, scratches his head, and says, "Hello? Hello? I need an ambulance—"

One duck walks into a bar and the   second duck ducks.

"My, oh my god, Anna?—Anna—Look at me honey come on my daughter she's been *hurt*"

"Thirteen thirty-eight Hoyt street she's bleeding, there's blood all over my"

"You do not understand it Needs to be here now we do not have time"

So the other patrons look at him and say:

Everything you said sounds great and if there's anything left to decide just tell me what to do.

Everything you said sounds great and if there's anything else just let me know what to do.

Everything you said sounds great, if there's anything else just let me know.

I've thought deeply about what you said.

I should say, I love it.

It's perfect.

It's terrible.

It's perfect, and terrible.

It's gigantic, terrible, and natural.

It's healthy, tame, and chemical.

It's idiotic, tame, and incurable.

It's harmless, helpless, invulnerable, and obvious.
It's happy defenseless moronic incurable excessive.
It's tame and misguided, despite that it's
Laser-guided, mean-spirited, helpful, and perfect.
It's particular and discrete
Meaning it knows exactly what to say and will never say it.
It's accessible, annoying, corrective, delightful,
erosive, flammable, heroic, inflammable,
kaleidoscopic and lost, missionary, mousy, nice,
nice enough, nicer, nicest, obvious, perfect, personal, polyamorous,
        polyphonic, queer,

it's specific: tagged as "teen" and "adult,"

incapable of being born

so you have thirteen hundred thousand eggs per day or thereabouts

which cost you ninety-three point six-four per thousand

all things considered

and which you can sell for ninety six something

it's so pastoral, so true. It's not a map, but it's accurate
                                        [it's not accurate]

it's the way the map melts over time
it's the falsified map, the map remembered
better than the city
and better than the city remembers its edges
it's the map of my heart

used to wrap up the real thing in avenues,
the map of the war, transparency map,

yes,

this is the map you were looking for

these maps you see before you are real maps of each other, just like
       reflections, like the reflections on a bottlefly's back
       in one thousand bottleflies. The word for "watch"
       is wrong, whereas the word "look" looks like a
       school. There is the newer pond, reflecting brighter
       and containing powerful fish. These fish have been
       leaping from the water and spinning all the way
       around eight or nine times, some of them have even
       suffocated. Those stupid fish, and those stupid
       other fish.
       And those happy fish, and those paralyzed fish,
       and those butterfly fish.

       And those fish that look exactly like dogs.

       All fish, crawling onto land, dragging
       each other.

       The way each seems to die and then doesn't is an
       everyday thing, as simple as *as*. You see a cloud
       of flies, metallic-green and thick.
                       Is it too real for you
       to really believe?
              Where we look like bits of thread
     and cotton,
         in this world beauty is so common.

table of CONTENTS

No, No, No

My form seemed to fill itself out
And I was happy
I ate well for three months, and then three months more
And when I woke up, I kept waking up
And it never stopped
I will trade you five hundred brain cells
And then I will use them to control you

The voice tears itself in half

Meaning being userside
Rather than serverside
You went to WAL-MART
And bought twelve skinned deer
Four hundred antlers
Shoplifted three sets of antlers
And gigantic condoms
To choke on

I imagine a deerhead yawning inside your throat
As chastisement
And I will open myself to you
Inside the words in French
Is the words in English

The tree curls above their heads and the river explodes

As divinity seems to manifest around their heads
I used that as an excuse not to talk about you
I eventually have to destroy Venice,
Geneva, and Istanbul
And there are some men talking
Watching themselves backwards in the pond talking

[

A drawing of a hand folding itself
and another hand pointing at you
sharing three of the same lines

]

The Exact Same Lines

Wandering from bedroom to bedroom and getting way too much sleep, she
Finds herself on a news report, missing. You can actually cause the consumer
To forget something he has previously learned by putting into his head
A bedroom, and placing into the bedroom a little doll of the thing, then having
The doll fall asleep. She soaks it in. Turns up the volume, *all* the way up,
Receiving *all* the signal, more signal than was ever broadcast, re-tuning her
Mouth to listen and her skin to watch, she soaks in it. For instance, let's say
Alicia hears a special report on a missing woman, a woman she knew as a girl,
And she thinks back to the times the two of them were falling asleep in separate
Bedrooms, every day of their lives, their dreams illuminated by the same
Radio waves, three dozen beds between them, entire gardens in their hands.
Alicia shows up

                in a new report on dreaming as Dreamer #3 and recognizes
Herself in it like a note recognizes a song. Dreamer Three reorganized her
Dream into a cascading series of bedrooms, populated with sleepy little dolls,
Sleeping. Soon the air between her and the television grows milky and ultra-
Pure, as she, Alicia, notices the front part of her head has drained into the
Television light, is stirring itself into the picture of her wandering out from
The screen, it's like you say "Hello" and so I, the consumer, say "Hello—

                              "right
Back. It's just that simple. You say you'll be back in about three hours and
We haven't seen you in a week? Do you see, Alicia, how much everyone
Sleeps when there's nothing on TV? She builds a to-scale
                            television doll, dresses
It up. She replaces the screen with an ultra-bright bulb, turns it off. Replaces the
Bulb with a garden, straddling it on the bed, thrusting handfuls of dirt into the
Special report on young, well-educated, employed consumers just vanishing,
Turning up dead—or worse!—the disappearance of Alicia Carter has residents

In this small community wondering whether this is another dramatic stunt or
Something far more tragic. For News 7, the

                                        room begins to get drowsy
around
            Us, the walls are barely hold

ing their
nails the

whole

room

blooms

        into two beds turning over in another bed, the room is composed leaf-
by-leaf between headphones, calculates total market share, I have access to at
least a couple bedrooms, hi, she, asleep, rolls over, there's vines pouring out of,
and doesn't feel, or feels but interprets the feeling so, your hair, so wrong, like
bottled water from a, the wriggling she, fake waterfall, which had nearly doubled
in the first, can't help but attempt, quarter two thousand ten, to use to escape,

                                                        the equalizer
                                                        boils
                                                        straight up
                            the garden   behind her
                            unfocuses its eyes   eyes/
                            the garden
the representation   unfocusing
overboard / over
lain over
actual

actual eyes. Alicia paints herself on

the television screen, strategy sort
of a mix

of eight songs threatening to replace the image
of bedroom with an image
of three
pillows subdividing into a swelling mosaic
mirrored
glasses
of water growing distant and
disaffected, the
third bar of the
song makes
you forget
the first two

as
a

news cycle

falling

asleep

in succession,

```
  *                           *
    *                              *
    *     *           *              *              *        *
  *           *     *           *                *        *
       *              *           *              *     *        *
  *     *     *     *     *     *     *        *           *     *
  *     *           *     *     *     *     *     *        *           *
  *     *     *     *           *     *     *     *     *     *     *
  *     *     *     *     *     *     *     *     *     *     *     *
  *     *     *     *     *     *     *     *     *     *     *     *
  *     *     *     *     *     *     *     *     *     *     *     *
  *     *     *     *     *     *     *     *     *     *     *     *
  *     *     *     *     *     *     *     *     *     *     *     *
  *     *     *     *     *     *     *     *     *     *     *     *
  *     *     *     *     *     *     *     *     *     *     *     *
  *     *     *     *     *     *     *     *     *     *     *     *
  *     *     *     *     *     *     *     *     *     *     *     *
  *     *     *     *     *     *     *     *     *     *     *     *
  *     *     *     *     *     *     *     *     *     *     *     *
  *     *     *     *     *     *     *     *     *     *     *     *
  *     *     *     *     *     *     *     *     *     *     *     *
  *     *     *     *     *     *     *     *     *     *     *     *
```

In those moments that feel inexact, as when just out of sleep you turn toward your lover and she reflects three of your lovers in aspects reflecting each other, or as when you open your eyes and the warmth on the bed sounds like a recording and your lover is looking at you the same way he looks at other people who aren't you, like then, in those moments

/

In those moments that feel inexact, feeling traces of other people inch across your skin and over your vision, you can almost, in that habitat of others' *is,* feel another's breath scraping yours from your throat and lungs, as when reading words out loud you really mean but did not write

/

In those moments that feel inexact even the fat lining your skin is breath and your brain, too, is breath, or the breath that comes in waves across your pillow seems of a kind with your vision and your eyes, and as you taste echoes of the breath you shared, each breath refracting and filling itself and the breath before it, each nerve the same noise

/

I cherish every moment, I was saying, recalling three moments at once and remembering them as one, but especially this one. We are together, in the same room. It is a bedroom, a bathroom, and another bedroom. At first the color has been taken from my clothes, and then the material, and then the pattern, is exactly how undressed we are.

And as we clothed each other in each other, scrambling our words and visions and smells, hazily there was something else there too, taking some lines and reciting them, and taking other lines and bending them, pulling us with an immersive gravity towards a certain story, and when I say this word instead of another word, and you say that word because it builds so nicely on what I said, and then we are speaking whole sentences we hadn't yet learned.

/

There are words that once you speak have bent you forever, grafted on to you or taken away from you irrevocably and irrecoverably.

You mean to say one thing, and you slip and speak a password, and the memory of that speaking soaks backwards from your mouth and drains down your neck, and fills you up to your skin with yolk, and these words are names, as all words are names.

I have named the moment you were in bed and didn't wake up until I had opened your pussy and pulled my body into yours, and your face opens up like a day on the road, and

I name that moment when I'm watching your face as you study me in the hotel shower and it feels like my sight has nerves, and that your sight touches mine, that it's drawing its fingernails through everything I can see,

I'm naming the moment we'll lie on the bed in a Y-shape, my arm between our faces, and your right eye will be hidden, and my left, and we'll share full knowledge of what each is looking at,

as we described the same thing in the same way, and became stained with the same word.

/

Since I left you, I was saying the only way to really know something is to remember everything else, as one will only know nakedness when they own no clothes, I am ceaselessly returning. You see one walk back in, and the next day another, and I begin to keep myself company inside you. They would all rather be the one arriving just now, watching your eyes draw your smile upwards, and soon there is another one here, still hoping to show back up, as one more and one more walk in and begin to mull around.

Of course, you remember them all as the one arriving.

Hi, you, you say.

/

[

three hands stemming from one another
in a way that does not suggest growth

]

He was whom, whom, whom, because of how deliciously the record was
spinning slow. But then his days go by without a thought in their head, and he
asks the camera, "So we can wish for anything? Anything at all?"

Still the stoplights change, cars hover at the margins like the charge in the
    socket, and
apparitions merge into material bodies at various speeds throughout the city,
the city my son was born in.

City of augurs, city of oracles, city of interpretations in this sense,
city arousing no carpet's harmonious pattern, city of divine origin,
controversy. City of similarities, come to the universe,
stained city, city that crumbles one upon the other amid clouds,
city shapelessly, city of streets, city of houses, of darkness,
city of graveyards. City titled, *The Wasteland and Other Poems*
by John Beer, Gucci Mane, and the nameless heart, by John Beer,
where Phoenix, Arizona used to be: is that what you've been
talking about, all along? Exactly what I wanted to hear?

I step outside at the moment of the first firework:
sound arrives like the mention of white rice,
and the city rosettes an otherwise tasteful sky.

Tasty city, city of raindrops slowed way, way slow,
to whom do you pray? When each thought you have
for a store, or a church, or a school stands up and
walks out, only to return some months or years later?

City which I will find until I am dead, sum city,
referred to in the third-person neuter, singular, surrogate
travelers shifting their gathering greens: all look down and speak of
trumpets, the streets trickling down the nerve endings of sampled voices:
the chorus of stepping outside.

Mother Russia, city of Petrograd, Leningrad, Stalingrad,
city of hermits, and, at times, the wind,

the pleasance, the pleasance, the pleasance, the pleasance, the pleasance,
the pleasance, the pleasance, and wind chimes, which disgust us,
because at this point we've got nothing else to feel. I felt like shattering
     the whole city
and the only thing that stopped me was you, and before I was all alone.
     Mother Russia,

Mother Russia, I find myself alone among these people,
and can ask nothing of them. The new abundance
is an assembly of dead bones, travelers, policemen.
Perhaps I have always been obsolete, and patient, waiting
with excitement in a crowd for an execution. Perhaps they
even roll a man onto the stage.
Naked except for modesty. Face obscured by a bag.

And now the sun has come out, which is so fine.
There is talk that a poem will be read, and that
announcements will follow. A warm wind seems to soften
even the children, who sit in the shade the crowd
stains onto the cobblestones. My son leans there, content to remark
     to his friend
about a schoolmate, stoop to examine an insect, or push his wrists out
     skyward
and curve his back to complement a yawn. The crowd itself could be an event:
its colors, noises, smells, yes, thousands of these, but also the potential,
concealed inside it, for revelation, for murder. This crowd

is not the event, not even to the women asking reasonable prices
for cigarettes and snacks, or to the sidewalk birds
who have displaced themselves to roof lines and lampposts.
You think you have discovered something, but really
you've missed out on so much. Even a couple of yards away there's
a play happening, with real live girls and boys and men and women.
Beyond that, a bus is exploding, and it's just like remembering something.
And past there is debris from the bus, having cooled so it can be moved.

But now my son has found you, and happily brought you to me,
but you are thirsty, and we shall smoke, and drink this,
what I have brought.

I watched the skin swallow him alive and retain its color.
Slowly applauded the creature that had been plaguing us all.
Now that it was in my power, the people proclaimed me

some kind of God. I grew long eyelashes and a fondness
for long eyelashes. The people only want an America
laid bare and wet, ankles tied to the collar, collar to the bed.

I realized I didn't care about any of it, least of all justice,
America, least of all all your justice. So sometimes we think
it might be a kind of game they're playing, the Afghan

Government and the American government, said Jalali.
The people are tired, and their hearts are tired.
Each one of them has fallen in love hundreds of times.

Some of them seem to fall in love every day,
and though this is not possible, there are many
who earnestly claim it. America, my people

are exhausted. I delight them ceaselessly with gifts,
blowjobs, and executions. They all want to give up.
The clouds on distant Chinese mountains still blind me,

after all this time, when I wait on distant Chinese hillsides,
carefully tending flocks of goats.
At night, I crucify one, then pray to it,

and pretend that that
is my religion
and in it I will never die.

And so I wait for death, and the moon finally answers
my many greetings.
My love for you is like an "untimely" death

and so I had shut my heart.
In the America of my youth, the moon was so bright
it's seared a crust on your eyes.

I love you so much that when I'm listening to your heartbeat I worry it'll stop.
Whatever I see in my heart, unannounced stop. With every new love he lets a
new line in,

fastens his heart to a new rib, explains the heartbeat.
He changes like a heartbeat, she accepts, the reservations are booked, it's
Paris, 1944, and he's been accidentally shot by a drunk corporal. She

stops. Regards
him. Hangs a sign on her heart asking for instruction. *We have come* so *far* she
seems to ask *and yet are refused a kinder stop?* If I could dance all night with
you

I would,

but it's Paris, 1944, and I've got dysentery, polio, and an inability to sigh.
I've been shot eight times, and have holes in my chest, both of my arms, one of
my hands, and my cheek, and there's an egg in my heart

with my heartbeat inside it. It's separated from the rest of my heart
by a thin white eggshell. Outside, it's all civilians. It's a shower of one man
presenting one woman with an expensive pearl necklace. *I'll feel happy* he
explains *you feel pretty.*

Outside, it's morning,

and the morning bells are ringing. Inside
is a yolk, hardening like a morning. Inside the yolk, the eternal soul

of a Spanish omelet.

It's mission bells multiplied by seagull bones, like a sub-woofer lain
beneath a xylophone, like that is how I love you, *te amo, Luz,* but I must die,
and you must go on, meaning it's morning,

Barcelona, 1924, and I've just been assassinated.
I love you so much that I am dead, and drifting through the long and fragmented
hallways of Spanish clouds, arriving out of air like shrapnel. I am dead,

his body explains as morning bells congregate around him,
but you mean so much to me I will die again. What you mean to me, and my death
means less, I love you more than me, and I

know what that means.

Even if we hadn't named it it was ours,
you might have understood my love

meaning, you might have understood my love,
whoever you are,

what you mean to me, though he die for it,
and tell them the secret, and die, what you mean,

if you'll allow me, what you mean to me,
the fear of death prevents me, and then to return,

and the father of thy children, die. What you
mean to me, and then to return, and tell them

the secret, and die. For if I did, I should die.
And in case I die, I paid one point two million

for this mausoleum, and you're telling me
it's only partially real? I paid a cool four

million for this airplane, and you're telling me
it's an angel? I spent a week's worth of food stamps

on a week's worth of food, and here we are:
shot to death in an electronics store? Smeared across

some new Iraqi highway? On the porch, electric green
from the reflected plants, imagining the blood clot

that stops the brain?

I pay the man and he goes, and I wait, and he comes back a little later wearing a name-tag. The name-tag says "Rainforest." I check it out, we nod, and I enter the rainforest, taking only knife, rope, canteen, and iodine.

Trees of every size with leaves of every shape slide and sift around me,
perfect butterflies soda around me
all around here.

Now, when one is in a survival-type situation, one is probably going to die.

It's important before entering a survival-type situation for one to ensure the life you have lived has been satisfactory.

It is important to set your affairs in order.

Call your loved ones before you, look them each in the eye, and die.

As you die, your soul will scatter from your mouth like confetti.

The confetti should hover there, two, three seconds long.

It would be nice if the confetti would subdivide into hundreds of small, bulbous confetti eggs.

And if each egg would then pop, and profess a rain of confetti all its own, like signals igniting the bush of undiscovered neurons.

So at this point, if there are hundreds of thousands of small confetti explosions, and you didn't have a chance for any last words,

. . . any last words?

It would be nice for your loved ones to find the letters you wrote them.

If these are just under your pillow, they will find them when they move your body.

It would be nice for this to be especially convenient.

Dear Woo,

When last I saw you, at the speech you gave, I listened mostly to your glasses, translating the flashes of the overhead lights across your pupils into a Japanese poem. This is a thank-you note. I need to ask you a favor.

The woman you know as Georgia is also known to me, though by a different name. She was involved with some of my interests in Georgia, and proved invaluable, though ultimately untrustworthy.

I take it you have not spoken to her of our correspondence?

Dear Emmett,

The way you leave rooms is
like you're entering another room, one
far more wondrous and colorful than which-
ever room I'm in, as if I can feel the needle of your
compass scraping away from
me and towards this magnificence.
I'm always happy to see you go.

I'm writing to ask you a favor, and I don't expect you to agree to it. But I expect you to get it done.

There is a box of bombs under your bed, most of which are mechanical, and the rest of which are spiritual.

Do you understand what I'm saying?

Dear Maribelle II

My lover, I have traded you for three Jeeps and a carton of shitty cigarettes.
This is just to say, I have traded you for a young sheep and a rifle.
I have cataloged your hopes.
I have observed you in the wild.
And now, I open a cage and you walk right in, greater than greater than.
Grand prize: eighteen sheep, three hundred charcoal-flavor birds, a Range Rover, and a hacked voting machine.
First prize: I take the muscle of your cheek and give you a new flag.
Second prize: I take away your flag.

Dear Rawling,

Nobody understands me the way I understand you. They can't even conceive of that.

You refer to every single thing by its correct name, but mean something different. It's the way a cellphone is a cellphone even thrown into the air, into smog, across the grass of ice in clouds, in stratosphere and space, in the act of being reeled slowly into the sun's field, readying itself to be crushed by gravity and burned into light.

It's nothing, really. Just a name, they say.

Friend, I'd have introduced you to so many people, but as they'd smile at you, and name you, their understanding of your name would be so incompatible with my understanding of your name, I'd kill us all.

I am so not fucking around.

Dear Selah,

I'm washing my mouth out, writing to you.

Assam,

Not hate, not an inability to find them cute, or charming, or things. Because there's going to be a baby in the backyard. And because the lambs hang low in the trees.

777	249	047	726
637	711	682	756
444	489	241	132

I am so not fucking around. Like a name strangling its body, I'll forget it, too. I'll say one thing, and then completely forget it. I'll remind you of something known to *everyone*: We could have gotten away with so much more.

For a letter to be any good, it's got to birth its own recipient. Assam writes a letter to Bri and must, that it be more fully received, show her her vulnerabilities and her beauties: all the invisible report.

    As he opens,

Dear Bri,

I'm so sleepy////   Shall we swim?

he invokes the moments before she steps into dreaming, delving running shapes and colors. These moments are when she most fits herself, her face blurry,

but her nerves blurry too, and lacing her image, worming up into it,

flattening her meaning into a skin interface,

Assam then lists recent episodes of pleasant acquaintance (excerpted):

> I think of being led by you through the stacks in Memorial
> Library [. . .] "the first to formulate the cult of tea as
> a sort of sacrament" [. . .] is this truly the first time,
> right now? [. . .] suicides at four Chinese factories [. . .
>] thrumming against the wet skin of your thigh, mouth
> pulled into mine [...] 'cross— that disguise— [. . .] the
> best time, again.

and places her image squarely in her chronology. This serves as his passport into
the shining and endless swimming-pool of her mind. His passport gets wet, and
there are few survivors, but at this point he's one of them, and her thoughts
have mistaken him for one of their own.

The ultimate desire of the letter-writer is to be orchestrator of a consensual tyranny: the voice inviting a specific mouth to a kiss, and the city-dwellers welcoming the men who will murder their Jews. The author is invited to and does provide perfect cosmetic surgeries, and so tailors the gland to swallow the message whole, or be cut to ribbons by it.

For instance, if Assam were now to write:

> Dearest Bri, the air is twice as deep, and
> yet I suck it down, for you, though I know
> it drown me.

The mention of air would chime with the heft of "actors" previously in the letter, to produce in Bri the sensation of clouds taking human shape, framing a school of bombers glistening there like lures. As you can see, Assam has timed this perfectly. Somewhere still in Bri's mind is the memory of Assam's erection thrumming so near her soaked pussy, and so Bri is reminded of a long muddy path cut into the city's grid: bombed-out, puddled, joyous.

Now, if Assam were to write:

> Dearest Bri, our meaning game is making designs in the sediment, some deep, and some floral, and some as light as lace-work petals lifting briefly in the heat of a fire.

or:

Dear Bri,

There's something you should know.
I'm guilty of everything.
The systematic diminishment of another. Supporting
a culture of sadistic and malicious violence. Captured
on video kicking a handcuffed inmate in the head. I
claimed most of the injuries were "self-inflicted"—
there were imprints of boot marks on the corpse, the
testicles were badly bruising and swollen. Inmates
bound in "restraint chairs." I was a champion of
excessive, unnecessary, and even purely malicious
violence. Incapacitating, deterring, and punishing,
with no intention of rehabilitation.

Race was one way of rationalizing my violent
domination. Another tape shows me pushing his head
forward on to his knees and pulling his arms back to
strap his wrists to the restraint chair. I order him to
get into the wheelchair. "I can't, I can't," he shouts,
"It hurts," and he's tasered on both hips, screams, still
can't get into the wheelchair.

I knew, on some level, they were all persons.

then he acknowledges every cell that divides within him is inside the scope of
God. In writing a letter to God, one should keep the audience in mind. One is
supposed to feel guilty. A good prayer is as a perfect vote would be. As gentle
and deep as the breeze across April

in waves as constant as corrective
as as.

As if instead of my version of the story, it was my version of the story injecting itself into episodes and commercials, a saliva inside them, as if to leach their bones. The heroes were interviewed relentlessly from birth. And if my version of the story shared gravity with the other stories, and with the audience. If it was a nexus, the neck from the brain on the body, between the sun and the sunrise:

Assam writes to Bri, and means to convey a very certain thing:

Dearest Bri,

In my last letter, I was distracted
but accurate.
I imagined and implemented a particular grammar
inside a system of meaning incommunicably specific. I
matched the words to my skeleton and crucified them
there, and was prophesied to die at a certain age, and
knew nothing could mean more than that. And yet,
here you are:

You are three sonnets fucking up
You are meat with Ash Wednesday skin
Next, you are learning unsolvable stations of the cross
Next, you are drinking blood and bone marrow
You are one little, two little, three little
You are a helpless item, and then you learn to crawl

first I boil meat in a pan
adding salt water every half hour
for hours

then I lose control and start
using my mind to control it and
make it cook

1: So why did you do it?

"2": I couldn't not. I had already been stretching out the phrases through misuse for about eight years? And nobody knew. But I wanted my whole earth carnage, I wanted my book to smell like a girl. So this was the next step. I always thought of myself like the executed princess. Like I wanted it more perfect but worse.

1: But—

"2": All conservatives are self-hating, and have no real desire, not even in love. Rather than lament it, I wanted to give them something so wounded, something actively trusting them completely because without immediate help it'll die.
    So it dies. That's what it was made to do.
    But after one of them gets a whiff of it, he'll chase it around his own
       head forever.
    So it gets better.

1: Many people seem to think your actions were politically motivated, which you deny. Have you read or seen any of these opinions? Do you have a response?

"2": Yes, all of them. Talk shows, tabloids, websites. I don't care who says it. Either you were there, or you were somewhere else.
    As for my politics, they're somewhere between cum vote and love vote.
    As for the assertion that I am politically motivated, I have no idea what that means.

1: Do you notice any differences between doing something alone by yourself, or in front of an audience, or with a small group of like-minded individuals performing for one another in front of congress, versus being part of the legislative body?

"2": Performing is the wrong word. I travel to alien, hostile cities in search of lifeless pink souls. All I find is rats. There's so many things in the world, but there's no souls, only rats. I have to wear lipstick to do this. And as for the rats, they were sick and the two ate the one and became ravenous, and then they ate each other.

[Q: Really?]

[A: Yes, eating each other.]

As a result, all I have for a sense of community is my all-purpose cup, a multi-tool, two donkeys, twelve feet of rope, and column after row after column of security monitors. All I have for "the audience" is the screen. That said, I still receive many letters, many from other elected representatives, letters from around the world.

Just yesterday I went with the mail to buy whatever sentiments stayed inside at the store. All the mail that arrived was raw meat, sometimes exponentially raw meat. The store was hot. The milk, I found out later, was rotten. But that was later. I left the store, holding the carton. I went home. I drank the milk. It was rotten.

The thing about the mail, by the time you get to the hallway mirror, the conversations you start with each of the letters that arrived—that's when I give you a real sugary look and follow you into the furnace.

In one version of the story, fire is a manifestation of pain: the victim, the life folded up in books. The story of fire is the consumption of the story: the book destroyed by the story, the story itself sparks . . . catches fire at the punctuation. In one story,

She says she wants to be killed that way. And
She
Really
Does.

He's a screwed-up messy fuck anyway, obsessed with feeling pain, talking about it online. In one version of the story, the fire travels unseen, as if burning backwards, as if predicting the change into ash and then forgetting it.

In another, it's a burning bush, but not an eternal flame.

In another, it's an eternal flame.

Dear tourist,

In my time, mountains slept in the distance,
and the noise from sheep and cattle being killed
drowned out our conversation.

Whereas the vegetable is content to eat the sun if it has to,

Dear Sun,

You're a bright and endless swimming pool
You're a great poetry reading, but in a bad way
You're a machine attached to a lung attached to a frog
You're leading a mission through the tall and endless forest of your hearing
Soon, you're inside a tight, Chinese-made piece of plastic for your face
This allows for maximum evaporation of tears

Finally, mountain environments, which are typically dry, also promote the
evaporation of tears.

Dear God,

I would call you. I can't but see my bank account reporting itself in the bottom of my vision. I call it Amanda McCauliff, a tall and monstrous blond of invisible cogs. I call her and get her to erase one of the overdrafts. All the names seem real similar in the same font. Like one, like two, like that.

So if you find the warmth of a palm on the back of your hand, if you seek comfort from even yourself,

imagine the name for your hand
that covers the other
is the name for my hand
in serif or in sans.

And if each time you read these words you spend that moment in time doing that forever, and each moment makes a new imprint and revises slightly the pattern, and each time the words lay their film of meaning over your revised thought the shape of the font impacts the pattern in lattice-work bruises,

if this, then
when I call you, and
name you, I mean

to make your shape
mine, and my shape yours.
Like this. Like that.

I think about a world in which the appearance of everything
becomes unplugged from all the things.
The grocery buying from the grocery buying,
the touching of an arm from the touching of an arm,
the drum machine from the synthesizer.
It'll look like everyone is walking around buying groceries
and dancing closely.
But only those of us who are sitting perfectly still will survive.
You see, unless you've memorized your whole environment,
unless everybody had,
everyone will be bumping into things and getting into accidents.
But you can survive by sitting perfectly still.

As at first the hours pass the shouting will quiet—
the shouting from under the soundtrack, where we are.

Our cellphones will work for a day or two.
And then we won't talk, but everything
will keep moving and sounds and images
will seem to be consulting.

There I am, we say, buying groceries, using food stamps.
There you are touching my arm and touching my hand.

And every so often, there we are,
appearing right here,
where we feel to be sitting.

And then there will be a time when we no longer think to anticipate this.

You stand in a movie set, tall fake trees all around you. You hear the noise of a
movie theater to the east, and electronic music from the soundtrack. Through
trees to the south you catch glimpses of an impressive mountain, Mount
Rushmore perhaps. A small dirt path starts up to the west and loses itself in the

darkness of dense fake woods. These woods continue to the north, blocking your passage entirely.

> N

You cannot go that way.

> E

You come to a **P S**

P.S. When you think about a world and the appearance of it has become detached from the world itself, I feel like you're almost my image wandering around far beyond my perception.

Dear God,

Thankfully this will be able to reach you.

Here is the list of questions that I am supposed to incorporate into my research paper. Any information is hopeful if anyone can email me back to let me know that I am not an emailing robot that would really help me a lot.

- I smashed my hand with the gauze on it into the table because it was hurting and then the blood would be dripping down my arm when it would reopen and I'd run at the small workers and attack them?
- Why is the economy so fucking *stinky* goddamn it?
- You're not hungry at all? (No I just ate)

Alana reads that humans are some of the smelliest mammals, that we've got odor-producing sweat glands all over us, and her mouth gets wet with the image of Pepsi. *The real thing,* she wonders, *the real one, you've got the true thing, baby. Oh shit*, then she goes into the bathroom, pulls the cord for the light, opens a window and goes in to work in tears. Similarly,

Cardiff stares at an anonymous spot on the floor for some twenty minutes, *but a lot of the meaning doesn't have names.* The door's been left open / someone driving by wonders about this. Well now, it's Rawling, his face filling the camera frame, pedal-to-the-metal, eyeballs set to China-time. *And when it has names it's always a little weird.* Cardiff is moving his toes unconsciously but gives them his full attention, and Alana, *Alana's having some fucking mess*, Rawling re-parses, *because what...? I'm smelly. Because she's smelly? Smelly, you've the, you're the smelliest of the real things, baby.* The floor is somewhere back in Cardiff's eyes, Alaina is rising like gel from Alana who is sniffing at herself in the shared bathroom.

Alaina reads the sign about germs and wonders why she can orgasm only with other people there, *is it their smell?* She walks out of the shared bathroom and into work really puzzled / into a bright and terrible room with one hundred men looking something like Cardiff, oh shit, she's feeling something quicken around her. Similarly, Rawling has miraculously not slowed down, he's actually going faster, the weave of traffic becomes still and clear and then he's got nobody around him, not roads soon, not even his cellphone signal can catch up— Rawling, faster than his clothes, meeting himself piece-by-piece, his sweat glands rolling off him, every skin-cell then every muscle-cell disintegrating, *Alaina*, he wonders at such a speed time slows down to last forever, *is having some fucking* melt*down, and what . . .? This means what . . . that what I gave to her was never made into meaning by her.* The Cardiffs are tapping nonsense morse code some three feet under their monitors, *or was mislabeled somehow*, and somewhere, just nearby, all over, the sale of the century is literally happening. . . .

- What is the apostrophe so fucking goddamn.
- So, say you have a million dollars—

Dear God,

- You've got A) a pinecone B) a A) a pinecone A) a pinecone B) oh. *no.*

Dear God,

- No?
- You're calling to say hi?
- Is that what that word means l-u-c-r-e?

No.

You take phonecall. You have: phonecall, a pinecone

You cannot drink phonecall.
You cannot wield phonecall.
You cannot sell phonecall.
You sell a pinecone. You've got:

For instance, everything is for sale in the UK, so your responsibilities may delay your responses to these questions, I would like to let you know that should I receive good responses from you I appreciated it.

Dear God,

Everything's for sale in the UK, even a name. But in the US where we do not have a strong sense of history and everything's run by big corporations (Big Pharma, Big Tobacco, Nintendo) everything is about Christianity and Muslims. And I wonder, what's the best part about heaven?

How does it (Nintendo) compare with death? (Complete:)

PRO: *Death is stronger than Nintendo, because in death you need no permission,*

_____

_____

_____

_____

CON: *Everything I can see is Heaven and Nintendo both,*

_____

_____

_____

_____

Rawling: In a way, death is the *perfect* story. It's like...

Anna: Like telling the story perfectly, in complete earnestness. As in: Here I Am. I Am Dead.

Rawling: Like heroes conquering death, that's the perfect story.

Perfect story:

The heroes come galloping through disaster and are forced to confront themselves. The main character begins losing motivation, walks to a nearby tree and sits under it. The scenery encroaches on the silence. Is this where we die? Perfect story:

Villains appear in the land like puberty. The sun is dangerously on fire. The hero is dosed with chemicals that will prevent him from ever being like himself again. Finding a nearby tree and feeling like he's got something to learn, perfect story: he cuts it apart, and it stops working.

Perfect story: In a city very much like the one you—you—live in, or one you grew up near, or a city similar to other cities, the heroes find themselves apart from each other and losing their memories. Baltimore saturates San Francisco. The dogs are wild dogs. The main character knows what she looks like in the mirror, finds a tree growing somewhere inside her. Soon the leaves are filling out her fingers, blocking her throat and pushing out her eyeballs. Her body explodes *and she's probably dead* and someone very much like her sits under the tree, thinking about himself.

Cardiff is thinking about himself as he plays the videogame. He is Adam, the first man, and he must collect bones to trade to the angels, and later he's got to go to the grocery store.

1) Adam, level 1, ass-naked and covered in mud leaps from the a palm tree and crushes the life out of the rabbit nesting beneath him.

2) Adam uses his teeth to carve into the rabbit's belly. He feels the warmth spray and pool over his tongue, skate down his jaw and neck and collarbone.

3) Adam spits out the rabbit's hip and leg and begins to pray over them:

"Dear—"

"Mask," says the rabbit's blood-soaked mouth, unexpectedly.

"Mask," says Adam.

"Miss," I said as she did something to the recording, "Miss—"

Look at you climbing the palm tree, I have a passion for fantasy books. And I get that, but at the same time, because in her books is where I could be best utilized. Counting when to, when to. Look at the braids in her irises, at the precision of eyelashes, at ellipses...

In one story, the man eats coins and falls to his death five or six times. There's another one with him eaten by orcs, and in another orcs are eaten by angels. My life feels more valuable every day. Myopia, utopia, an unhealthy fantasy life and a spreading bank account like a wave of learning-to-count children. She steps on her own toe. Butters her voice-box. She's one big tulip in a tulip shop.

Stepping over versions of herself, she imagines *on* them and *up* them, she directs the man through a series of increasingly realistic rooms and cities. I feel useful, the man means, gaining levels. And from her hands and wrists through her bones to her lungs, all her breath feels useful, as her name is remembered better every day by even her friends and lovers; as she appears more over all the world the world seems so familiar. I buy clothes for myself in the story.

I clothe myself in the story, its soundtrack leeching into my tongue like a molecule. Accomplishing a Tuesday, and then a Wednesday, and then a Thursday. She steps out of the closet the absolute picture of clothing.

(*enter* Angela, *wearing a schoolgirl outfit—plaid skirt, bone-white blouse, a pencil behind each ear and one suggestively dangling from her lips. Her shoes, it should be said, have some blood on them*)

Angela: Do you like me like I like to, when I, you know...

Cardiff: You like I'm meeting you here once more, one more icing of you on you.
Angela: You like me, washes like me over me like a breath that's water.

Cardiff: Your water when, like when I wish to learn

[

　　　　　When I imagine other people learning
　　　　　I imagine them learning to be more

Like me

                                                                ]

                            pouring my vision over you—

(enter Angela *wearing a pencil-thin red bikini, golden body-paint up to her eyelids and generally making a mask out of her skin)*

Angela: Gosh, Cardiff! Well this is how I feel, so this is how I look!

(Cardiff puffs off in a steam of smoke and anger, frowning, framed for a crime he can't wait to commit, following--wait--steaming over hills... like, through the dressing room...

Cardiff: *stolen from the rich,* Cardiff, *wired his money up in smoke, and he wears it like clothes, or he wears it like stolen clothes rather)*

(enter Angela *dressed in a hundred million dollars)*

Cardiff: I'll pay you a hundred thousand dollars for it—

Angela: Aw, Cardiff, are you—

Yes,

The movie is exactly about hope and despair, and hope and despair listening to each other and so infecting each other, brainstem via cochlea via voice . . .

For instance, say I deliberately limit my speech, I go so far as to only ever say this one thing, regardless of circumstance or stimulus. Let's say I say *I say*. Surely *I say* "I say" means something different to me today than it did yesterday. Let's say it gains meaning, mumbling it in bed means morning *I say,* speaking it in front of the camera always a coda of the moment. So

I say

Dear God,

In regards to your honesty, I think the poorest of the poor deserve it the most,
and then the second-poorest.
God, they will listen.
Show you their rare affection.
Like adding thickener to your tears.
In regards to your honesty, toughing out the economy.

You see, it's a shame and the future is all a goddamn mess, it is awful I'm here
to say! I see one way and then I see another, and there comes this point that all
you're looking at is looked at through tears.

They fall silently from flowering trees in a late spring snow.

God, my darling girl-cat lost today, and though it fought long battles with diseases
it was devastating to both of us. She didn't die alone. I was here the entire time.

We were so connected,

Rather than try harder to reach you, I have opted into a new plan for communication:

Really Speaking Your Heart.

The thing is, in reaching you thus, if your heart doesn't recognize the product of mine, well who's to know? For instance, if I were to put it into song:

but I sang it at so high a frequency only children would hear it, sure I'm being honest but am I being honest to you?

For instance, I really love it when newscasters fuck up!

And when I'm in love with someone and I sometimes feel like that, like totally fucking up! "Excuse me"s and connector words containing nothing of the whole beast I feel because it wouldn't let one part of itself away.

And someone's likely to not understand at first; when they do understand am I then communicating honestly?

Or when I'm talking to someone in love yes but hoping to be overheard too, but then I'm into that kind of intimacy.

X

O

Wait.

[Appendix: Alice Fulton]

She actually put her heart *inside* of your heart *inside* of my heart!

"She's kicking, ohh! Oh, she's kicking!"

Alice Fulton is in the freezer! She can't get out! Mally and Lucy put her there, just to see. Now they're pushing against the freezer door, hooting.

"Come on Alice Fulton," yells Mally, "put your fingers in the ice cube tray!"

"Come on Alice Fulton," yells Lucy, "put your feet in the bag of ice for parties!"

She has clay-colored skin that looks like wet clay when she steps out of the shower / and into the bright and terrible room.

All morning and afternoon she draws her fingernails up
and then down
and then up
and then up
and down my heart, hello, this has been exhausting!

And in front of the moon in deep, glorious summer, once three layers of sweat have formed on our skin and been reabsorbed, I lean into her, grab her hair at the roots with my right hand, put my left hand over her hand and kiss her!

"Hello? Rawling!" says Lucy, who has now got one foot up on the fridge as she's pulling on the handle to the freezer, "A little fucking help?"

"Come on out Alice Fulton," yells Mally, "we know you're in there!"

And as we kiss, her lips are pulled into mine, and her tongue from between her lips, and from her tongue her heart is pulled into my mouth like a thick, knotty minnow.

Now, the pumping of the heart is inside my body, but it's not specifically *for* me.

And as my saliva begins to digest it, the heart continues to pump / but like the heart of a forest full of crickets . . .

Accordingly, I was granted that which I desired most, and I took it. And when I was asked to explain myself, I no longer had to. The guards had lost any desire to capture me, and the bankers had donated their sperm to the relief effort. Actually, the money was then used to buy *me*, from *you*. You now feel an overwhelming, denaturing sense of loss. Thus. A little later, three hundred thousand versions of me swarm into you like drums, and you are pregnant now, with my three hundred thousand children. That which I desired most, the three hundred thousand yous is now acceleratingly three-point-three hundred thousand yous / screaming thirty-three hundred million names for me / through your shorting synapses. Dear God, thou givest and you give, and a little later, well, you get back. Here is a word of power. There is a word retreating. Now, a word reeled back in to the bottom of my stomach and concealed like a pearl. Now, every word is a name / and every name is a note, / U, U, / stacked like cups inside your shape and your mind. As in: every part of every cell has inside it the shape for every cell. Honestly, that which I desired most was a more marketable solipsism: your name pasted onto everything, when every word is the same prayer, and all language holy. No, three thousand thous and three thousand yous stacked like glittering identities in the sunshine and melting. Door cleaves open.

[Appendix: Diagram of Writing Paper and Dying]

Anjie's talking to him about her boyfriend, Cardiff, in a way obviously meant to lead him on, that I'm writing a research paper on? As I research and bibliography, Anjie takes his hand without any warning, puts her hand over his, actually locking himself outside the submarine. His own speargun had ripped a hole in his wetsuit in the battle with the squid, but the keys were gone. And re-research, and re-bibliography. He wants to, in that i-dunno way, though there is almost no information publicly available on my research paper, to touch her shoulder? In my research paper on my research paper, most of my facts are guesses, some documents are stolen, Cardiff is no good, she says, I wish I could be with a nice guy. Now something just like death is in my paper, and I didn't put it there. He says, well, Cardiff is just difference in communications, he says, well, Cardiff is just bad at communicating, Anjie, now death has entered my paper. Because he got back to the submarine with an eighth of a tank of oxygen, he was stupid, naturally heroic, and it begins pacing the sentences with me, I write a sentence, but it sounds like maybe, and in an across-the-street way, you two aren't, death writes a sentence, fully compatible, too. Anjie draws her hand back, and turns away. Rawling, she says, I'm sorry. He's what I like, you don't understand. He was exploring an underwater trench and drowned, you want to hear how he died?

You don't understand, God,

I understand so little and the world's a mystery I'm here to say! The world is one huge intimacy—

I forgive you, God,

I forgive with my eyes closed. He walks up, I close my eyes, and forgive. She's already forgiven me though she doesn't know it. Forgive me, I forgive you, after all. I close my eyes and then it's only hearing and then I go deaf. It is then I forgive you.

But inside my forgiveness there's something different too. I close my eyes, she walks up, she plucks my forgiveness from somewhere and it's like there's a seed inside it. Or an egg. She does something else, I forget exactly, but she puts it to her open mouth, closes her eyes, bite forming in her mind—

You find yourself standing in a forest with your eyes closed. The trees here are primarily oak and palm, and > inventory

You have:

Head:	Golden-black hair
Body:	Golden body paint
Right hand:	Palm
Left hand:	Rabbit skeleton
Feet:	Black loafers (bloody)

You find yourself standing in a forest with your eyes closed. The trees here are making a low humming noise, and you hear five and then four and then three cascading series of quick clicks and whiffs as insects take off and land in the grass around you. You feel another set of eyelids closing over your own . . .

Democrats have run inner cities, public schools, universities, unions, manu-facturing, black churches, for decades, all bamboozled, I mean hardcore Hollywood Democrats,

[my beautiful friend]

You are not blatant against the Democrats and regulations, openly attacking like open health care markets, like abortions and housing loans, like open ERs killing hospital budgets.

[come with me]

I know, but it's got to be more!

[looking for it]

Bring more direct accusations of Democrat failures like inner cities, universities, more exposure of school textbooks, of force-fed Hollywood Democrat issues to their fullest. If they want MY issues or if they want condoms in schools, if they want inner cities, public schools, manufacturing, then get a law allowing kids to have sex at home! I think the future is going to be awful! Like universities, unions, black churches,

[should we stop looking?]

What do you think: MORE attacks against Democrats, or allowing kids to have sex at school, open ERs and hospitals!

[looking for what?]

Rather than try harder to reach you, in reaching you such, if your heart

God, if your heart shows up late,

I showed up almost two hours late and surprised everyone. The string of ancestors in my wake was singing to me a song I could hear through my shoes. Their names were floating inside them and seemed to filter something from their voices. Surprise, I said, I'm late. Sunshine was all around. Sticky embryonic sunshine.

I showed up almost two hours late and surprised everyone, Surprise! I said, I brought beer and all the great books and television shows, I'll show, I show you what it means to be surprised. I mean *really* surprised!

I surprised myself two hours late and surprised everyone. And feeling surprised I woke to all the websites and all the television shows, and what the sun looks like on television. Like, whoah! Surprise, God!

And in the matter of broken hearts, divinity. No,
Serenity.

And in the matter of broken hearts, let's get better and try harder
and erase all the things that we find only in ourselves.

My back's in the grass. The sky is my stationary.

I write to you with love in my heart and hand and
my eyes and my teeth in my hand and my heart in my mouth
bleeding down my face.

Dear God,

I appreciate your movies, and then appreciated them again. Folding one film inside the next I came to know you, and I came to love you, and I came to write to you, with my mind and my hands handshaking to do so. I don't think I'm important, and I don't resent that you are.

I know a lot of people think the world is already a wasteland, and there are others convinced it'll soon become one. Every generation of Christians since Jesus has creamed for the Second Coming. But you, your charm is staying classy in the face of despair. It's an indulgence in style just for the joy of being beautiful, God, beautiful God, call me information.

This is paradise. And this is where the poor people live now, in these towering movies. One's called *Own Nothing*; after all, God provides for the birds, and does he not love thee more? One's called *Enter the Void*, and one's called *A Collection of Poems*, as if we get to keep them.

In the movie of having nothing, even the scenery is empty, and no one speaks.

It is not a silent movie. It is a violent movie.

Dear Diary, it begins, Dear Social Anxiety,

Should I tell her? That I'm thinking about telling her? That I just thought about whether I should tell her that I'm deciding to tell her or not? And if you

do tell her, how much of the deliberation should you include? "I decided I should tell you," you might say, "if you'll listen—and, you, I know you will!—"

but for the soundtrack that first trickles, then pours from every available leaf and

audience, and soon it's flooded, a deluge that fills you even to your ozone,

when even the prayers ferment, one wave, one saline shot of come, one

sentence swelling and bursting into panspermia, a firework, prismatic eyelash, void of your iris.

Perhaps it is fate that today is the Fourth of July,
and inevitable in the course of history.

And once again you are fighting for your freedom,
like in the movie *Independence Day*.

In less than an hour, you will die.
Perhaps it's fate that today you shall die,

that you will lose, and that it's today
we should meet,

and like this.
We're going to live on,

but not you, America,
no part of you will.

Your endless seashores, mountains, etc.
will die, all of your skies,

all your flags.
America,

they'd rather live underwater and drown
than put up with more of your ecstasy.

The endless roads all end in the sea
as surely as the rats do.

America, mute informant,
pulse of the goat, America,

the slowest surgery,
the flowering land of God,

I eat all your words
and turn your children into knives.

"In one version of the game," "No referee in no other sport was so able to do so right by a game," "the winner sits the next round out. In another, the winner chooses the next winner." "while remaining so completely anonymous to his audience." "**Q**: When does a game stop being a game?" "The Sport with the Most Organized Judicial System" "and in another, the winner is never revealed." "You must defend your house, and you get a gun to do this." "There's good reason games have rules and judges—why there's so much fun to be had in the world bisected by limits."

"Joining the referees is joining a team." "So much comfort, too." "Their job is to remain professional in an emotionally charged situation." "**A**: When it can refuse to stop being played." "One side is 'shirts' and the other is 'skins.'" "Something as specific as the pass interference rule becoming common knowledge." "To do so, they must learn to trust each other, and accept each others' judgments."

"He was born at Detroit Mercy Hospital, and was a die-hard Detroit fan his entire life." "If a referee suspects another referee of taking sides," "He wed Amanda at twenty-four and she soon bore him three sons." "Before the game, everybody's mind is on the game," "they will speak privately after the game," "as if magnetized by the plural object."

"The rules of a joke are like the rules of a game:" The baby is pretending to be an egg, but it takes a mother to notice that. "There's the baby," the mother and father notice, "and only in the most extreme cases will the league be notified." "pretending to be an egg/soccerball." "You guys be skins."

"When I was a child, I spoke as a child," "There's the starting position/set-up," "I felt as a child, and I thought as a child." "the development of that position,"

"But when I became an egg," "and various opportunities for reversals." "No you guys be skins." "I put away childish things, was fertilized, died, and was buried, and grew up into a chicken dinner."

"So the game ends, and each player thinks they lost. When really, one of them didn't."

The inaccurate echo

Be in the way the description of glittering will sometimes cause it. You will step into a chamber, hold on to a support bar, and while stretched across the bardo of auditory hallucinations after the moment of death. One of us says the lights and the other shatters them. Steps into the chamber, puts on the headphones, the reflection of the whammy bar. The way you talk about me to me.

Unquote echo

You find some new fortune in between the light's curve and blinking. Corporeal, edged, acoustic. Tied up to the bedposts, the way I use your eyelids is like it just occurred to us to ask us, want to have a kid together? But what can you use them for but suffering. Shelter them. Holocene. Ellipses in eclipse, the stars are all the Story of Fire. The way / you rise to work / and/or / every night, in person or apart, I know we'll fall asleep together.

In those moments that feel inexact, as when just out of sleep you turn around and fall back, immersed in evening, when you open your eyes to watch yourself open your eyes and the warmth of the bed feels like a record melting over your face in slow-mo sunlight in late June, and suddenly you really want to breathe, like then, in those moments

/

In those moments that feel inexact, when you feel the signature of another star on your particular estate, you can almost, in that habitat of foreign space/ time, feel another god clawing its way from deep inside your mineral, up your lungs and throat, as when reading words out loud you really mean but did not write

/

In those moments that feel inexact even the skin lining your shape, even your mind, mine, is the dumb drift of breath across wind, across the window, across your bedsheets and the seams of your headspace, and as you thrum with the echoes of my word, a reflection pinballs, repurposes the architecture, refracting through the exact same noise

/

She notices you noticing her. You notice this, like normal, but then you notice something new: she knows how you think. What you're thinking. No. The nameless machines of your thoughts, she knows them as intimately as you do.

Yes. It's sudden.

Scenery is just sitting there like always, and light is no different, splashed down the walls of buildings to the concrete, and people scattered about seem not to be aware that something is happening, and she's somehow developed in every wrinkle of the inside of your head. But not an image of her. Her herself. That's her over there inside of here. And it took no time at all.

These are her thoughts too.

You find yourself all over her head, riding the synapses of her vision, feel the lick of her eyelid across it, and you recognize the expression on your face from her eyes, and you've seen that somewhere, just a second ago, on someone else's face.

/

The heat of her tongue seals your eyelids, but her saliva seeps in anyways, something about it does. Your eyelashes and skin cells filter the liquid out of it, the taste of her taste, take away the saliva itself. Her meaning of it arrives in your vision ultra pure.

It's not what you hoped. What you hoped for was so much smaller, provincial, ridiculous. What you hoped for was washed away when the first drops hit the cortex. What she means has nothing anymore to do with hope. The city of her experience spreads out before you, unfolds into more folds into street leading into alley into doorway into bedroom by bedroom by bedroom.

/

Morning reveals itself—the sequence of nudity—
sheds lovers and cities petal by petal.
A thin sheet covers her legs.
Her vision fills the room.

/

for Rachel especially

for pleasant animals and warm plants

for prayers to angels, eternal gardens of feathers

for all the audiotape inside the earth, tangling like roots

for ten thousand dollars you would swallow this book and what else

for creosote, gasoline, drive-shifter, gasoline, chlorine, drive-shafts, wooden doilies, chamomile, gasoline, grenadine, sheaves of doves, creosote, gasoline, and wood-oil

for I remember the second time I recited the poem to you
for I remembered the children-voices I was going to do
for intimacy is inherently sudden

for Abby
for Allyson Alyssa for Phoebe and Andrea for Melanie for Julia Linda Leslie Christina and Trinka, for Nico, forgot Margaret but, ultimately, for everyone, really, this is all our doing, running in a fog of saturate light, in love, in emulsion, in love, in situ, in kif and in keeping with the thought of the mix, in thigh-high socks, in twelve-by-twelve pixel blocks breaking like breakdowns in likable
    foreign pop, in Tame Impala, in alpha thru amygdala and on to in media res, pink cotton etceteras, etcetera, from the humble drum machine, from graveyard surcharges, from learned apes, an endless phonecall, from an endless phonecall, a signals marinade,
        from the sweetness of the initial comes the calorie of the name,

for I arrived three hours late and surprised everyone of my dreams, my diagram, my chemistry, from my canonical accomplishments to Crater Lake, Oregon, Maddelyn High and I at The Farm Cafe and Farm and I at The Saz in Madison eating hummus and feta,

for foods, etc., and for the sake of universal justice I dedicate this to you, eternal justice and food, "I parade in my parade costume," a love-letter italicized, forever and ever, for from the fashion of your vision comes the manner of your face,

for the time you said capital-d Delighted: a promise to think about it until I'm dead
from graveyards come funerals, come find out with me,

in-depth audience interviews administered bi-monthly
for from wet noise comes tea leaf bound into folio, it is a gift of time we give inherently, actively, ceaselessly, mom, gosh,
for al-Abracadabra, alpha-beta, for to be afraid of illegal love, instead, I live as a nun and a martyr:
from sunrise unto sunspot and belly-up again in holy dawn, prayer daily restored, virginal, polite, apolitical as far as economics and in love with the slim figures come through my window, early morning familiars, when the mission bells come

within the air itself, undilated yet fully full air
with bells, bells, silver bells, sudden bells
increasingly soggy over hours and then years one null note over and ever and under and over again additionally

increasingly loud, admittedly mass-produced, come in, come in,

it is amazing out there—

for I am Leviticus or one of the others

for I am alive to prove it

for I love the fragrance for its neck, and the stem for its vein

> *for I need no shield*
> *for I need no shield*
> *for I need to walk eighty ways and back*

thru each scale

> *and to name each note its position to*

the sun / and the sum / of earth's accomplished / spin

> *for when I lose myself I make damn sure*

it was something I needed

> *for the insurgents in the good book:*
>
> *a new end:*
>
> *they want / no armor*

THE MOTHERWELL PRIZE
Negro League Baseball   Harmony Holiday
living must bury   Josie Sigler
Aim Straight at the Fountain and Press Vaporize   Elizabeth Marie Young
Unspoiled Air   Kaisa Ullsvik Miller

THE ALBERTA PRIZE
The Cow   Ariana Reines
Practice, Restraint   Laura Sims
A Magic Book   Sasha Steensen
Sky Girl   Rosemary Griggs
The Real Moon of Poetry and Other Poems   Tina Brown Celona
Zirconia   Chelsey Minnis

FENCE MODERN POETS SERIES
Eyelid Lick   Donald Dunbar
Nick Demske   Nick Demske
Duties of an English Foreign Secretary   Macgregor Card
Star in the Eye   James Shea
Structure of the Embryonic Rat Brain   Christopher Janke
The Stupefying Flashbulbs   Daniel Brenner
Povel   Geraldine Kim
The Opening Question   Prageeta Sharma
Apprehend   Elizabeth Robinson
The Red Bird   Joyelle McSweeney

NATIONAL POETRY SERIES
Your Invitation to a Modest Breakfast   Hannah Gamble
A Map Predetermined and Chance   Laura Wetherington
The Network   Jena Osman
The Black Automaton   Douglas Kearney
Collapsible Poetics Theater   Rodrigo Toscano

ANTHOLOGIES & CRITICAL WORKS
Not for Mothers Only: Contemporary Poets on Child-Getting & Child-Rearing
– Catherine Wagner & Rebecca Wolff, editors

A Best of Fence: The First Nine Years, Volumes 1 & 2
— Rebecca Wolff and Fence Editors, editors

POETRY
A Book Beginning What and Ending Away   Clark Coolidge
88 Sonnets   Clark Coolidge
Mellow Actions   Brandon Downing
Percussion Grenade   Joyelle McSweeney
Coeur de Lion   Ariana Reines
June   Daniel Brenner
English Fragments A Brief History of the Soul   Martin Corless-Smith
The Sore Throat & Other Poems   Aaron Kunin
Dead Ahead   Ben Doller
My New Job   Catherine Wagner
Stranger   Laura Sims
The Method   Sasha Steensen
The Orphan & Its Relations   Elizabeth Robinson
Site Acquisition   Brian Young
Rogue Hemlocks   Carl Martin
19 Names for Our Band   Jibade-Khalil Huffman
Infamous Landscapes   Prageeta Sharma
Bad Bad   Chelsey Minnis
Snip Snip!   Tina Brown Celona
Yes, Master   Michael Earl Craig
Swallows   Martin Corless-Smith
Folding Ruler Star   Aaron Kunin
The Commandrine & Other Poems   Joyelle McSweeney
Macular Hole   Catherine Wagner
Nota   Martin Corless-Smith
Father of Noise   Anthony McCann
Can You Relax in My House   Michael Earl Craig
Miss America   Catherine Wagner

FICTION
Prayer and Parable: Stories   Paul Maliszewski
Flet: A Novel   Joyelle McSweeney
The Mandarin   Aaron Kunin

 has a mission to redefine the terms of accessibility by publishing challenging writing distinguished by idiosyncrasy and intelligence rather than by allegiance with camps, schools, or cliques. It is part of our press's mission to support writers who might otherwise have difficulty being recognized because their work doesn't answer to either the mainstream or to recognizable modes of experimentation.

For information about our book prizes, or about *Fence,* visit www.fenceportal.org.